To _Travis_

May this gift help
strengthen your faith
and light your way.

From _Betty_

Little Book of Faith

CONTRIBUTING WRITER
GARY WILDE

PUBLICATIONS INTERNATIONAL, LTD.

Gary Wilde is a full-time freelance author and editor who has written numerous books, educational materials, and magazine articles on religious and self-help issues. Some of his books include The Bedside Book of Prayer and God's Daily Inspirations, a perpetual calendar. One of his ongoing projects is editing the devotional quarterly Quiet Hour.

Photo credits:

Front & back cover: Clifton Carr

Thomas Braise/The Stock Market: 47; Clifton Carr: Front & back end sheets; **Index Stock Photography, Inc.:** Wallace Garrison: 61; Robert Houser: 11; Picture Perfect: 25, 35, 41; **G. Randall/FPG International:** 21; **Tony Stone Images:** 26; Jerry Alexander: 33; Rob Boudreau: Contents page; Nick Dolding: 67; Sylvain Grandadam: 77; Sara Gray: 68; Darrell Gulin: 17, 37; Pal Hermansen: Title page; Gavriel Jecan: 71; Richard Kaylin: 38; Charles Krebs: 53; Matt Lambert: 14; Charles A. Mauzy: 13, 58; Brigitte Merle: 57; A. Milliken: 55; David Muench: 75; Marc Muench: 29; Ian O'leary: 62; Stephen Studd: 8; Art Wolfe: 73; **SuperStock:** 23, 48.

Contents

INTRODUCTION
The Beginnings of Faith — 8

CHAPTER 1
Search for Peace — 14

CHAPTER 2
Entering Solitude — 26

CHAPTER 3
Encountering the Awesome — 38

CHAPTER 4
Surviving Tough Times — 48

CHAPTER 5
Knowing Joy — 58

CHAPTER 6
Hoping for the Future — 68

The Beginnings of Faith

Now faith is the assurance of things hoped for, the conviction of things not seen. Indeed, by faith our ancestors received approval. By faith we understand that the worlds were prepared by the word of God, so that what is seen was made from things that are not visible.

—HEBREWS 11:1-3

Cultivate Your Faith

The apostles said to the Lord, "Increase our faith!" The Lord replied, "If you had faith the size of a mustard seed, you could say to this mulberry tree, 'Be uprooted and planted in the sea,' and it would obey you."

—LUKE 17:5-6

FAITH IS THE touchstone of your relationship with God. It is a great and glorious experience when it is sufficient, and can seem like our undoing when it is not.

With practice, faith is as simple as taking a breath. Today, believe God for one small thing—it will be the beginning of your walk of faith.

Lord, teach me to walk by faith, whether with baby steps or giant strides.

Trees and Seeds

The kingdom of heaven is like a mustard
seed that someone took and sowed in his
field; it is the smallest of all the seeds, but
when it has grown it is the greatest of shrubs
and becomes a tree, so that the birds of the
air come and make nests in its branches.

—MATTHEW 13:31-32

In a field of dark earth,
a humble hand plants a mustard seed.
Tiny, it seems of little worth,
sown in spring; a deliberate deed

performed from the heart—
with Heavenly elements to feed,
and faith no small part.
The planter feels this need.

So small, but strength is inside.
Green shoots soon start—
leaves broaden, reach high.
Yellow flowers unfold, now living art!

Support from spreading roots
   underground—
steady breezes; branches arch,
like the reed—hidden strength is found.
Weathering strife; time builds bark.

The Creator knows this divine art.
For He sees an autumn tree first,
where once only a tiny seed laid stark.
With faith, trees will cover the earth.

Perfect Faith

THERE WAS ONCE a man who had a perfect life—in fact he often mused on his many blessings and personal successes. During one of these moments he questioned whether there was even one thing wrong with his life. His answer loomed large.

There was a mountain at the back of his house. It was lovely mountain, but it blocked his view of the Pacific Ocean. Being a spiritual man, he decided to pray for the mountain to move, trusting in Matthew 17:20: "...if you have faith the size of a mustard seed, you will say to this mountain 'Move from here to there,' and it will move; and nothing will be impossible for you."

So he decided to pray for one month, morning, noon, and night, that the mountain barring his view of the Pacific Ocean would move. At dawn on the

appointed day he awoke early, ran to the window and threw up the shade, only to find the mountain still there.

He tore down the shade, stamped his foot, and shouted "I knew it!"

Imagine having perfect faith: Never questioning God's plan for us, never asking whether he really loves us. But the important element of faith is knowing that we may not have perfect faith, but we have faith in a perfect God.

CHAPTER 1

Search
for Peace

This stillness feels like
your presence, dear Lord.
This hum in the air,
your gentle breath.
This sunlight,
your purifying touch.
And this peace—
the kind only You can give—
reaches far past my understanding.

Material . . . or Meaning?

> Vanity of vanities, says the Teacher;
> all is vanity.
>
> —ECCLESIASTES 12:8

KING SOLOMON, the Teacher, had everything. However, he discovered a soulful meaninglessness behind every new acquisition. Focusing on one "thing" at a time, as he was doing, never brings lasting satisfaction. There is always the eventual letdown, when the new becomes the old. Perhaps this desire for meaning, combined with its absence among the things of earth, means it must be found somewhere else. This was Solomon's ultimate conclusion, one that leads beyond the merely material.

May I remember today that ultimate meaning in life can only come from the Ultimate Being.

In Silence, Listen!

Drop thy still dews of quietness,
    Till all our striving cease;
Take from our souls the strain and stress,
And let our ordered lives confess
    The beauty of thy peace.
Breathe through the heats of our desire
    Thy coolness and thy balm;
Let sense be dumb, let flesh retire;
Speak through the earthquake, wind, and
        fire,
    O still small voice of calm!
—JOHN GREENLEAF WHITTIER, 1807–1892

Let me listen for heavenly guidance amidst the noise and confusion of my day, and even in the quiet—keep me attentive.

Toil, and Time To Rest

The appetite of the lazy craves,
and gets nothing,
while the appetite of the diligent
is richly supplied.
—PROVERBS 13:4

A QUESTION we all face: How can I maintain a better balance of work and rest in my life?

"I suppose I work so hard because I don't want anyone to think I'm lazy," Larry commented to a friend. But his friend, and most everyone who knew Larry, were more concerned about something else: They hated seeing Larry become a workaholic!

How is it with you? Have you found the daily satisfaction of weaving together diligent work and intentional inactivity?

Satisfy my appetite for accomplishment through adequate toil, and time to soak in the required energy.

Peace Through Patience

Better is the end of a thing than its
beginning; the patient in spirit are better
than the proud in spirit.

—ECCLESIASTES 7:8

Spinning your wheels today? When
we're disturbed about our work "going
nowhere," seeming to produce so little;
when caught in a routine of drudgery or
an endless round of boring routine . . . we
can stop to consider: *What long-term effects
may come of this?* After all, many jobs don't
show immediate results, such as child-
rearing, planting trees, or community
organizing. And, of course, a time of bore-
dom or dissatisfaction can be good for us.
How else could we develop patience?

*Today let me approach my work in patience, recogniz-
ing that my efforts could have far-reaching effects that
I'll never witness.*

1 9

Not Yet Perfect

> Very truly, I tell you, you will weep and
> mourn . . . you will have pain, but your pain
> will turn into joy.
>
> —JOHN 16:20

IN A PRESUMABLY perfect world, there would be no depression, no suffering, no pain, not even any death. But this brave new world would be lifeless. It would be static and pointless, full of a hypnotically dull and relentless sameness. If we all had perfect bodies and perfect minds, the joy of individual difference and mutual discovery would disappear. We would know exactly what to expect. . . .

—LESLIE HAZLETON

Knowing that perfection isn't an option, I will seek peace and joy amidst the good times and the hard times—all the times that make up a full life.

The More Things Change...

What has been
is what will be,
and what has been done
is what will be done;
there is nothing new under the sun.
—ECCLESIASTES 1:9

WHAT A FAST-PACED, constantly changing world we live in! Does anything ever stay the same?

Yes! When it comes to the inner life—the essential needs and longings, the motives and goals of us all—these things have always been the same, and will remain so.

For just a moment, I'll recall that the undercurrents of my spiritual life flow deeper than this stormy, wave-tossed surface.

Don't Change a Thing

...there is great gain in godliness combined with contentment...

—1 TIMOTHY 6:6

FOR SOME PEOPLE, the idea of peace means to dull the awareness, to relax into a state of unconcern, or to take up a simple, mind-numbing chore. There is a place for these things, but suppose we regularly tried increasing our attentiveness to reality, rather than trying to escape from it?

Rather than diverting our minds with the latest in entertainment, instead of daydreaming or taking a nap, suppose we held our gaze steady for a few moments each day, simply focusing on what is *real*?

Imagine: No judgment about the things that can't be changed. No clinging to the things that are lost and can't be found. No longing for what has been, but will never be again.

Simply accepting what is.
Now.
Concerned with the reality of the only life we have. Just for a moment; a cadence without judgment. And not having to make it different or better, in any way.

In gratitude for what is—all of it a gift—could we not find peace?

Since all the aspects of my existence come down from Your gracious hand, I will take a moment to survey the goodness of my life, just as it is. Amen.

CHAPTER 2

Entering Solitude

Under all speech that is good for
anything there lies a silence that is
better. Silence is deep as Eternity;
speech is shallow as Time.
—THOMAS CARLYLE

A Quiet Examination

Search me, O God, and know my heart;
test me and know my thoughts.
See if there is any wicked way in me,
and lead me in the way everlasting.
—PSALM 139:23-24

IN SCHOOL we had to do it all the time: Take quizzes and exams. But even after graduation, our lives are full of tests that show us how well we're progressing.

Have you considered the need to "examine" your spiritual growth occasionally, too? We can do it during our times of solitude. In those quiet moments of contemplation, we can rummage back through our days to discover areas of our lives that still need "heavenly repair work."

As I think back through my days, show me how to learn from my mistakes and benefit from recognizing my unwise choices.

27

Alone, Just "Be"

After he had dismissed the crowds, he went up the mountain by himself to pray. When evening came, he was there alone...

—MATTHEW 14:23

WE HAVE CLEARLY lost something when we are no longer free just to be, when we must always be active, doing some things and refraining from doing others. Something is missing when we have to force our pauses, carve out our spaces, and then feel we have to justify them. As a result, recreation often means engaging in more pleasurable work, not freedom from having to work at all.

—GERALD MAY

Let me welcome into my day the times of solitude, those precious moments when I am most receptive to your fellowship, my Ever-Present God.

Let Love In

For I am convinced that neither death, nor
life, nor angels, nor rulers, nor things
present, nor things to come, nor powers,
nor height, nor depth, nor anything else in
all creation, will be able to separate us from
the love of God in Christ Jesus our Lord.
—ROMANS 8:38-39

"WHAT DO YOU DO all day?" a friend
asked an elderly woman living alone.

"Well," she said, "I get my hymn book
and sing. Then I read the Psalms, meditat-
ing on God's greatness. When I get tired
of reading and can't sing anymore, I just
sit still and let the Lord love me!"

Not even our aloneness can separate us
from love. Solitude can be an adventure in
spiritual growth, rather than another problem to be solved. Is it that way for you?

How can I know Your love, unless I experience it?

First, the Emptiness

For God alone my soul waits in silence,
for my hope is from him.

—PSALM 62:5

THE CHRISTIAN WAY of life does not take away our loneliness...Sometimes it seems as if we do everything possible to avoid the painful confrontation with our basic human loneliness.... Our loneliness reveals to us an inner emptiness that can be destructive when misunderstood, but filled with promise for him who can tolerate its sweet pain.

—HENRI NOUWEN

Teach me, Lord, that emptiness must come first—the prerequisite to being filled with Your presence and peace.

Silent Knowing

But the LORD is in his holy temple;
let all the earth keep silence before him!
—HABAKKUK 2:20

HAVE YOU EVER stood, perfectly still, in the middle of a forest, just listening to the silence as the sun comes filtering through the leaves?

"The food of the soul is Light and Space," said Herman Melville. And we need that kind of nourishment, the solitude that brings us into a holy sanctuary. There we stand in stillness on the brink of the absolute, a place no longer just for seeing—but a place of knowing, too.

Nourish me, God, as I welcome this gift of quiet time and space, opening my soul for a morsel of Your goodness.

Opportunity to Move Closer

Turn to me and be gracious to me,
for I am lonely and afflicted.

—PSALM 25:16

THERE IS A TENDENCY in each one of us to
deny loneliness. We want to live life inde-
pendently, not leaning on other people.
But a nagging sense of loneliness keeps
getting in the way. Sometimes it becomes
so severe we can hardly think about anything else. I believe God created us in-
complete, not as a cruel trick to edge us
toward self-pity, but as an opportunity to
edge us toward others with similar needs.

—PHILLIP YANCEY

*If I am lonely today, I will let my need for others move
me closer to a potential friend.*

Face It!

You desire truth in the inward being;
therefore teach me wisdom in my
secret heart.

—PSALM 51:6

WHAT IS SO frightening about time to be
still and alone? Is it that we may have to
take a reckoning of our defenses? We
avoid ourselves because what was hidden
just below the surface may pop up and
demand response. How inconvenient!

If I rush through my day, my selfish
frenzy seems natural. If I'm despondent
over deadlines, my bickering with the
kids or co-workers appears justified. And
if I've accomplished "important" work all
day, then my escape in front of the TV all
evening may feel like a deserved retreat.
Unless...

Unless I choose instead to be quiet; to
listen to myself. Then my self-indulgence

becomes less reasonable. It may take on the look of rather shallow escape tactics.

For some of us, the negativity in quietness is dwelling on our "symptoms" and thinking that we are falling short. But consider: Perhaps your well-honed defenses are simply becoming more and more apparent. Good!

The human spirit is the lamp of the LORD, searching every innermost part.
—PROVERBS 20:27

What might become apparent to you if you took a moment—right now—to listen to the whispering of your soul?

CHAPTER 3

Encountering the Awesome

God moves in a mysterious way,
His wonders to perform;
He plants his footsteps in the sea,
And rides upon the storm.
—WILLIAM COWPER

Yes, He's Here!

**The LORD is near to all who call on him,
to all who call on him in truth.**
—PSALM 145:18

YOU'VE NO DOUBT had a "shock" like this
before:

"When the line pulls at your hand,
when something breathes beside you in
the darkness. . . . It is always shocking to
meet life when we thought were alone."
—C. S. LEWIS

Don't be shocked. The God of the
universe is as close to you as your breath.
Don't be shocked. Simply become
aware . . . and call on Him with all your
needs.

*While "maintaining" our religion, let us pause and
consider: The living God is really here, truly available,
ever so close, always.*

Yes, You Do Pray

Listen to the sound of my cry,
my King and my God,
for to you I pray.

—PSALM 5:2

WE ALL PRAY, whether we think of it as praying or not. The odd silence we fall into when something very beautiful is happening, or something very good or very bad. The ah-h-h-h! that sometimes floats up out of us as out of a Fourth of July crowd when the skyrocket bursts over the water. . . . Whatever words or sounds we use for sighing with over our own lives. These are all prayers in their way.

—FREDERICK BUECHNER

Thank You that communicating with Heaven requires nothing more than an open heart. Amen.

Whose Power?

Have you an arm like God,
and can you thunder with a voice like his?
—JOB 40:9

"IT'S JUST the angels bowling," said the little boy, no doubt repeating an often-heard bit of parental wisdom intended to keep the child from fearing those massive peals of thunder.

But why wouldn't any of us be afraid? The threatening rumble, reverberating deep within our chests, is truly awesome.

Yes, we ought to feel small in the face of it—and blessed. For we are reminded that we are not the most powerful of all beings in the universe. Wouldn't it be sad—and even more scary—if it were otherwise?

The awesomeness of each storm is a potent, practical invitation to know the presence and power of the Holy.

The Gift of Duty

They show that what the law requires is written on their hearts, to which their own conscience also bears witness...

—ROMANS 2:15A

HAVE YOU NOTICED the sense of "ought" that human beings carry within them from birth? It's a feeling of moral obligation, of duty, bordering on guilt. No doubt it's the reason we find worship of some variety in every culture.

Suppose we were to ask ourselves: *Where does this inner sense of obligation come from?*

How would you answer? Religious people say it's built into creation, because creation has a moral Creator.

But how would you answer?

The next time I take up some duty, let me offer thanks for my sense of duty—an awesome gift.

43

Keep it Balanced

For as the heavens are higher than the earth,
so are my ways higher than your ways
and my thoughts than your thoughts.
—ISAIAH 55:9

. . . I have called you friends, because I have
made known to you everything that I have
heard from my Father.
—JOHN 15:15B

WE CAN VIEW spirituality as friendship
with God. As we do so, these two
themes—God is holy and God is personal—must both be held in our minds,
existing in a dynamic tension.
—JAMES OSTERHAUS

*Today I will approach You, as a friend, knowing that
even my greatest problems are nothing compared to
Your power.*

Look All Around!

The heavens are telling the glory of God;
and the firmament proclaims his
handiwork. Day to day pours forth speech,
and night to night declares knowledge.

—PSALM 19:1-2

EVERY ONE of us has had experiences
which we have not been able to explain:
a sudden sense of loneliness, or a feeling
of wonder or awe in the face of the uni-
versal vastness. We were forced to sus-
pend our acquired doubts while, for a
moment, the clouds were rolled back and
we saw and heard for ourselves.

—A. W. TOZER

*When I confront the mysteries of this life, may I
remember that the unexplainable may well be a
conduit for the Holy.*

Call Now

Seek the LORD while he may be found, call upon him while he is near.
—ISAIAH 55:6

YOU KEEP trying to get through, but the phone is busy. You keep calling, but the answering machine continues to intrude, a lifeless human surrogate.

In our busy world it's not uncommon to come up short when trying to reach people—everyone seems to be on the move. Many people just aren't available during the day. They're tied up with work, taking a vacation, or just determined to stay out of touch.

The prophet says we must seek God while He is near. What a strange statement! Does it mean that we sometimes take God's availability for granted?

Yet there is a perfect time to call upon the Lord with all of our pressing needs

and important messages—and that time is now.

No doubt God is always, in some sense, "available," for we are assured of His constant presence. The past and the future fade into obscurity; the present moment is the only guaranteed "response time" we have.

None of us knows that we will be available for the Lord in the week or year ahead—or even in the next minute.

Lord, I call upon you now . . . please draw near to me, and I will not back away.

CHAPTER 4

Surviving Tough Times

My help comes from the LORD,
who made heaven and earth.
He will not let your foot be moved;
he who keeps you will not slumber.

—PSALM 121:2-3

In Weakness: Strength

Three times I appealed to the Lord about
this [affliction], that it would leave me, but
he said to me, "My grace is sufficient for
you, for power is made perfect in
weakness." So, I will boast all the more
gladly of my weaknesses, . . .

—2 CORINTHIANS 12:8-9A

If iron sharpens iron,
    then knock, with holy sparks, upon
        this dull heart.
If trouble shapes character,
    then let this trial be my daily bread.
And if absence makes the heart grow
    fonder, then I dare even say:
Remain hidden a bit longer,
    painful as it may be.

*When we feel weak, it can be a sign of blessings to
come. Here, after all, is the opportunity to invite God's
power into our lives.*

Bad, With Good Effects

O LORD, how long shall I cry for help,
and you will not listen? . . .
Destruction and violence are before me;
strife and contention arise.
—HABAKKUK 1:2-3

OUCH! Time to see the doctor. Whenever pain cuts into our lives, we want to find out exactly why.

But the question of suffering goes deeper: Why does it exist at all, especially in a world God loves? Habakkuk, God's prophet, wrangled with the Almighty about this and received a pretty straightforward answer about the divine plan to set things right—eventually.

We know that pain is bad, but it can have good effects—growing our own souls, and calling others to compassion.

What Now?

My brothers and sisters, whenever you face
trials of any kind, consider it nothing but joy,
because you know that the testing of your
faith produces endurance; and let endurance
have its full effect, so that you may be mature
and complete, lacking in nothing.

—JAMES 1:2-4

THE MOST extraordinary thing about the
oyster is this. Irritations get into his shell.
He does not like them. But when he cannot get rid of them, he uses the irritation
to do the loveliest thing an oyster ever has
a chance to do. If there are irritations in
our lives today, there is only one prescrip-
tion: make a pearl.

—HARRY EMERSON FOSDICK

*Dear God, show me how to let every event of my life
be a means of growth—even if it's simply the progress
of patience and perseverance within me.*

Looking Beyond the Temporary

**God gives burdens,
also shoulders.**

—YIDDISH PROVERB

WE ARE AFFLICTED in every way, but not crushed; perplexed, but not driven to despair; persecuted, but not forsaken; struck down, but not destroyed; . . .

So we do not lose heart. Even though our outer nature is wasting away, our inner nature is being renewed day by day. For this slight momentary affliction is preparing us for an eternal weight of glory beyond all measure, because we look not at what can be seen but at what cannot be seen; for what can be seen is temporary, but what cannot be seen is eternal. —2 CORINTHIANS 4:8-9, 16-18

When burdens overwhelm us, before trying to change the situation, let us first seek to broaden our vision.

Working How?

THEY SAY THAT God is at work in all the circumstances of our lives—even the painful ones. Of course, that's not to say that every situation is a good one, or even that it will eventually result in goodness. Surely sickness and death are on God's list, too, of bad things that happen among humans.

So exactly how is God working here? Let us imagine one small way and try to be content with it now: Painful events in our lives produce in us empathy and compassion for others in similar pain. And the world could do with a few more ounces of those holy virtues.

God is at work in this suffering world, always at work to evoke a bit more compassion—starting with me.

Nothing Can Separate Us

Where there is sorrow, there is holy ground.
—OSCAR WILDE

WE KNOW that all things work together for good for those who love God, who are called according to his purpose. For those whom he foreknew he also predestined to be conformed to the image of his Son, in order that he might be the firstborn within a large family. And those whom he predestined he also called; and those whom he called he also justified; and those whom he justified he also glorified.

What then are we to say about these things? If God is for us, who is against us?... Who will separate us from the love of Christ? Will hardship, or distress, or persecution, or famine, or nakedness, or peril, or sword?...

No, in all these things we are more than conquerors through him who loved

us. For I am convinced that neither death, nor life, nor angels, nor rulers, nor things present, nor things to come, nor powers, nor height, nor depth, nor anything else in all creation, will be able to separate us from the love of God in Christ Jesus our Lord.

—ROMANS 8:28-31, 35, 37-39

Thank You, Lord, for the promise of Your constant, loving presence through every tough time I will ever face.

CHAPTER 5

Knowing Joy

I can hardly contain this joy,
Dear Lord.
Like a river overflowing its banks,
I'm gushing, too—Celebrate! Dance to
the music!
Astonished, suddenly, I recollect:
It's merely a foretaste.

How to Be Happy

But let all who take refuge in you rejoice;
let them ever sing for joy. Spread your
protection over them, so that those who
love your name may exult in you.

—PSALM 5:11

Happiness is like a butterfly;
The more you pursue it,
The more it eludes you.

But when you turn your attention
to other things, it comes,
And sits gently on your shoulder.

—NATHANIEL HAWTHORNE

As I go about my day, I will let happiness land where it will, in its own time and place.

Blessed—By Giving

> ...we must support the weak,
> remembering the words of the Lord Jesus,
> for he himself said, "It is more blessed to
> give than to receive."
>
> —ACTS 20:35B

THE EPITAPH on an old gravestone reads:

What I gave, I have;

what I spent, I had;

what I kept, I lost.

Isn't it true that the only things we really own are the things we've given away? What would it mean for you, then, to loosen your grip on a few favorite possessions? Would it be worth a try to find out if it is, indeed, more blessed to give than to receive?

As I give, may I seek more contentment—with less left over.

Joy Through Loving

What does love look like? It has the hands to help others. It has the feet to hasten to the poor and needy. It has the eyes to see misery and want. It has the ears to hear sighs and sorrows. That is what love looks like.

—St. Augustine

If I speak in the tongues of mortals and of
   angels,
   but do not have love,
   I am a noisy gong or a clanging cymbal.

And if I have prophetic powers,
   and understand all mysteries and all
      knowledge,
   and if I have all faith,
   so as to remove mountains,
   but do not have love,
   I am nothing.
   If I give away all my possessions,
   and if I hand over my body so that I
      may boast,
   but do not have love,
   I gain nothing.
                    —1 Corinthians 13:1-3

*Thank You for reminding me: There is no joy for myself
if I am always by myself. Help me spread happiness by
spreading love, every chance I get.*

What Do You Think?

Finally, beloved, whatever is true, whatever
is honorable, whatever is just, whatever is
pure, whatever is pleasing, whatever is
commendable, if there is any excellence and
if there is anything worthy of praise, think
about these things.

—PHILIPPIANS 4:8

COMPUTER programmers live by this
technological truism every day: "Garbage
in, garbage out."

But doesn't that little rule apply to the
human mind, as well? If so, we must
constantly ask ourselves: Do the things I
think about help me grow spiritually and
make me a more joyful person? What
about the kinds of attitudes I'm harbor-
ing right now?

*As the seed-bed of character, my attitude—moment by
moment—makes all the difference.*

Your Choice!

Be strong and courageous; do not be
frightened or dismayed, for the LORD your
God is with you wherever you go.

—JOSHUA 1:9

"I HAVE a new philosophy," said *Peanuts*
character Charlie Brown. "I'm only going
to dread one day at a time."

To what extent is fear robbing you of
joy, day by day?

It helps to remember: Fear can lead to
good or bad. For example, fire can either
warm our hands or burn down our house.
So fear can either launch us into problem
solving and loving action, or it can cause
us to run away or lash out in rage.

*Thankfully, we can decide what to do with our fears,
and our choice will make all the difference.*

Content, No Matter What

...I have learned to be content with whatever I have. I know what it is to have little, and I know what it is to have plenty. In any and all circumstances I have learned the secret of being well-fed and of going hungry, of having plenty and of being in need. I can do all things through him who strengthens me.

—PHILIPPIANS 4:11B-13

"MONEY CAN'T BUY happiness, you know," said Jessica.

"Well, I'd like to try being rich and unhappy rather than poor and unhappy," said Juan, as he stared at the negative balance in his checkbook—once again.

Have you been there?

We may agree intellectually with Jessica. However, we still long for just a little bit more in the bank. But when will we arrive at the place of "enough"? It seems

we never get there. Perhaps we can learn
from the apostle Paul's statement. He'd
been there, too—both rich and poor—
and had learned to be content either way.
Not that it was wrong to be rich or partic-
ularly noble to be poor. It's just that, for
him, the bank balance was a side issue.

He knew that in the tough times, God's
love would shine through his life even
brighter.

Yes, he was content with that. Are you?

*Lord, loosen my grip on money today, and free me to
ponder details that will last beyond my bank account.*

CHAPTER 6

Hoping for the Future

For surely I know the plans I have for
you, says the LORD, plans for your
welfare and not for harm, to give
you a future with hope.

—JEREMIAH 29:11

Critical Decisions

Listen to advice and accept instruction,
that you may gain wisdom for the future.
—PROVERBS 19:20

IF YOU'VE EVER waited for a subway train,
then it's likely happened to you: The train
stops and suddenly two doors open at
exactly the same time—with you stand-
ing halfway between them.

Did you freeze for a moment, or
maybe do a "dance," on your way first to
one door and then the other? (Or maybe
you laughed at someone else doing this
indecisive little jig.)

Life is full of important choices. Have
your choices allowed the light of God's
wisdom to show through in the critical
decisions you've made so far?

*In every choice I face today, may I keep my ears attuned
to heavenly guidance.*

Light of Wisdom

Know that wisdom is such to your soul;
if you find it, you will find a future,
and your hope will not be cut off.
—PROVERBS 24:14

This window-light diffused in prism hue
shows me how You penetrate my heart:
in tones of joy and sadness,
in jubilation and grief.

Enter once again with Your great wisdom!

In every bright, white moment
or grey routine,
in all your invisible splendor
be there—always—
coloring the days of my life.

I need Your wise guidance, Lord, to enter the future
with confidence and peace!

Big Change Coming...

Listen, I will tell you a mystery! We will not
all die, but we will all be changed, in a
moment, in the twinkling of an eye, at the
last trumpet. For the trumpet will sound,
and the dead will be raised imperishable,
and we will be changed.

—1 CORINTHIANS 15:51-52

"BUT WE'VE *always* done it that way." It's a
classic line.

Why is change so difficult, even when
we're doing God's will? And even more
daunting is the challenge to let go of
some personal habit or secret desire that
is hindering our spiritual growth. What is
it for you? Are you ready to change?

*No matter what small change is required at the
moment, let me keep in mind the big change coming at
the end of time.*

Always There

And remember, I am with you always,
to the end of the age.
—MATTHEW 28:20B

As the rain hides the stars,
as the autumn mist hides the hills,
as the clouds veil the blue of the sky,
so the dark happenings of my lot
hide the shining of thy face from me.

Yet, if I may hold thy hand in the darkness,
it is enough.
Since I know that,
though I may stumble in my going,
thou dost not fall.
—ANONYMOUS CELTIC PRAYER

I believe in You, God, even when it is hard to discern
Your presence.

Who's Leading Now?

The LORD is my shepherd,
I shall not want.
He makes me lie down in green pastures;
he leads me beside still waters;
he restores my soul.
He leads me in right paths for his name's
  sake.
Even though I walk through the darkest
  valley,
I fear no evil; for you are with me;
your rod and your staff—they comfort
  me.
You prepare a table before me in the
presence of my enemies; you anoint my
head with oil; my cup overflows.
Surely goodness and mercy shall follow
me all the days of my life, and I shall
dwell in the house of the LORD my
whole life long.

—PSALM 23